THIS BOOK BELONGS TO...

Name: Theo **Age:** 10

Favourite player: Deleg Eu/Deeng

2019/2020

My Predictions...   **Actual...**

The Hornets' final position:

The Hornets' top scorer:

Premier League Winners:

Premier League top scorer:

FA Cup Winners:

EFL Cup Winners:

Contributors: Steve Scott, Matt King, David Anderson, Kevin Newman & Peter Rogers

A TWOCAN PUBLICATION

©2019. Published by twocan under licence from Watford FC.

ISBN 978-1-912692-53-8

£9

WATFORD

4

CONTENTS

WATFORD

Heurelho GOMES

01

POSITION: **Goalkeeper**   COUNTRY: **Brazil**   DOB: **15/02/1981**

The former Tottenham Hotspur goalkeeper looked all set to retire at the end of last season. He played what were expected to be his final games for Watford in the fantastic FA Cup run on the way to the final, including a very emotional display against Crystal Palace at Vicarage Road, but subsequently decided to stay on for another year.

Daryl JANMAAT

02

POSITION: **Defender**   COUNTRY: **Netherlands**   DOB: **22/07/1989**

Janmaat battled it out with Kiko Femenía for the right-back spot last season, with both players enjoying extended runs in the starting XI throughout the campaign. The Dutch international likes to get forward and got six assists in his first 34 appearances for his country, while he also represented the Netherlands in their last World Cup finals campaign in 2014.

THE 2019/20 SQUAD

Craig
DAWSON

04

POSITION: **Defender**   COUNTRY: **England**   DOB: **06/05/1990**

Dawson joined the Golden Boys from West Bromwich Albion at the start of the season, reuniting with his former Baggies teammate Ben Foster. He is comfortable playing as either a centre-back or auxiliary right-back and is an aerial threat from set-pieces. The former England Under-21 international, now 29, also represented Great Britain at the 2012 Olympics in London.

Sebastian
PRÖDL

05

POSITION: **Defender**   COUNTRY: **Austria**   DOB: **21/06/1987**

The 6'4" centre-back was one of the first signings made by Watford after their promotion to the Premier League, joining on a free transfer after his contract at Werder Bremen had expired in July 2015. The Austrian was a regular starter for three seasons, scoring three goals and helping the Hornets establish themselves as a Premier League club.

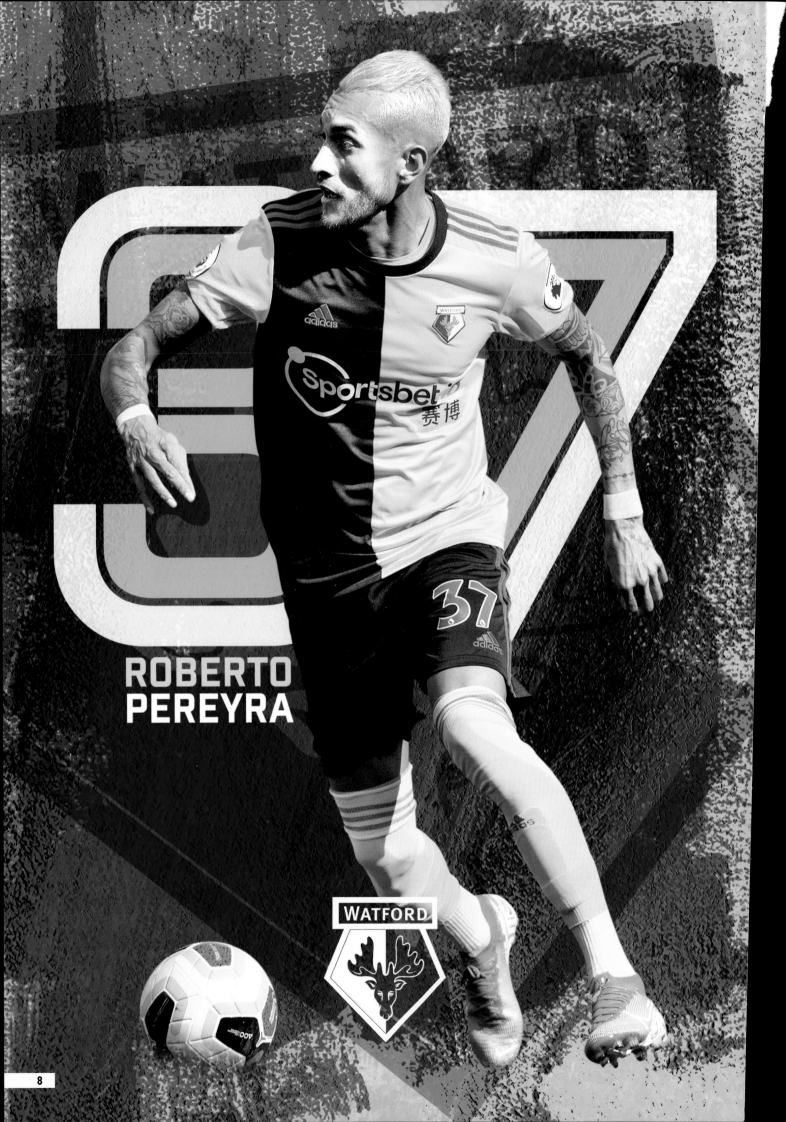

ROBERTO
PEREYRA

THE LEGEND
ALEC CHAMBERLAIN

1. THE BREAKTHROUGH

Restricted to just four games during his first season at The Vic, 'Chambo' was ever-present the following year as Watford secured the Division Two title in 1997/98. His inspired form in the Hornets' goal earned him the Player of the Season trophy, but his journey was just beginning.

2. SPOT-KICK SAVIOUR

On a long night in Birmingham, Chamberlain wrote himself into Watford folklore with two penalty saves that earned Watford a tense shoot-out win in the 1998/99 Division One Play-Off semi-final. First he denied ex-Hornet Paul Furlong, then he made the decisive save from Chris Holland to send Graham Taylor's men to Wembley.

3. BOLTON BEATEN

Chamberlain proved his semi-final heroics were no fluke as an inspired display in goal helped Watford achieve promotion to the Premier League. The keeper's stunning save kept out an early Eiður Guðjohnsen chance and set the foundation for a famous 2-0 Play-Off final win over Bolton at Wembley.

4. PLAYER OF THE SEASON

One of few positives in an otherwise difficult 2001/02 for Gianluca Vialli's Hornets, Chamberlain played understudy to Espen Baardsen right through to late October, when he made the first of 35 straight appearances. He never looked back, excelling in Watford's goal and ultimately picking up his second Player of the Season award.

5. FAREWELL 'CHAMBO'

With retirement just around the corner, a 42-year-old Chamberlain made his first and last appearance of the season - and the final outing of a fine career - as a late substitute for Ben Foster on the closing day of 2006/07 against Newcastle. It was a fond farewell, but 'Chambo' was to stick around for a further ten years on the club's coaching staff.

WATFORD

GERARD DEULOFEU

2018/19

GOAL OF THE SEASON

10

WATFORD 3
WOLVES 2 (AET)

FA CUP SEMI-FINAL
SUNDAY APRIL 7, 2019

It was always going to take something sublime to top what was the Hornets' strongest Goal of the Season shortlist in many a year.

There was Will Hughes' rocket against Fulham, mazy individual efforts from Roberto Pereyra and Gerard Deulofeu in wins over Huddersfield and Cardiff, and who can forget Domingos Quina's pair of pearlers against the Bluebirds and Reading?

That's just to mention five of the 15 fantastic strikes nominated, with Watford supporters given the difficult task of choosing which goal would succeed Daryl Janmaat's 2017/18 winning effort against Chelsea in an online vote.

But in the end, there was only ever going to be one winner. Deulofeu's audacious curling chip in the FA Cup semi-final against Wolves was not only high in quality, but even higher in significance.

Described in a tweet by Gary Lineker as 'exquisite', this piece of magic that inexplicably found the top corner from the tightest of angles inspired one of the greatest comebacks the FA Cup and Wembley Stadium have ever seen.

Previously 2-0 down with little more than ten minutes remaining, what had seemed a lost cause was now anything but, and a newly-inspired Watford went on to salvage a dramatic late equaliser - via Troy Deeney's stoppage time penalty - before that man Deulofeu popped up again to win it in extra-time.

Not bad for a player only introduced from the bench with 25 minutes to go. The Hornets had reached their first FA Cup final in 35 years, and in some style.

Adrian
MARIAPPA
06

POSITION: Defender   **COUNTRY:** Jamaica   **DOB:** 03/10/1986

Mariappa made 32 appearances last season, enjoying consistent runs in the first team in the absence of Christian Kabasele. The defender came through the ranks at Watford's Academy, playing in the Premier League and captaining the side before leaving to join Reading. But the popular figure made his homecoming in 2016 and slotted comfortably back into life at Vicarage Road.

Gerard
DEULOFEU
07

POSITION: Forward   **COUNTRY:** Spain   **DOB:** 13/03/1994

After an impressive loan spell in the second half of 2017/18, Deulofeu joined the Golden Boys permanently ahead of the 2018/19 season and has so far proved an excellent signing. In 33 appearances last season, the former Barcelona player scored 12 goals and wrote himself into the club's history books with a heroic performance in the FA Cup semi-final.

Tom
CLEVERLEY
08

POSITION: Midfielder   **COUNTRY:** England   **DOB:** 12/08/1989

Injuries restricted Cleverley, who signed from Everton in March 2017, to just 17 appearances last season, but he did score a vital winner in a 2-1 away victory at Crystal Palace in January. The tireless midfielder has 13 England caps and represented Great Britain at the London 2012 Olympics. He was previously at Vicarage Road on loan during the 2009/10 season and was named Player of the Season.

WATFORD

Troy
DEENEY
09

POSITION: Forward   **COUNTRY:** England   **DOB:** 29/06/1988

Fan favourite Troy Deeney has been at the club since 2010 and is already a Watford legend. The 31-year-old striker scored eleven times in 37 games in 2018/19 and led his team to an FA Cup final. Known for his physical style of play and vocal leadership, the captain is widely known for his dramatic winner in the 2013 Play-Off semi-final against Leicester City.

THE 2019/20 SQUAD

D Wears the Birmingham City captain's armband

E Crystal Palace's nickname

F Danish Head Coach at Griffin Park

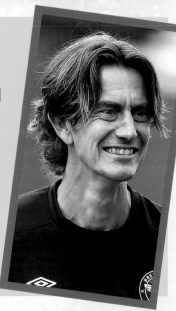

A Chelsea's Spanish skipper

B Do you recognise this Championship club's crest

G The Toffees play their home games here

H Longest serving Championship manager and a Millwall legend

C Scored the first home league goal of the season at the City Ground

I Foxes' Nigeria international signing who wears No.8

WATFORD

A Z

2019/20 PART 1

WHO'S WHO &
WHAT'S WHAT
OF ENGLISH
FOOTBALL?

J Manchester City's Brazilian striker who was part of their 2019 Copa América winning side

K Polish international midfielder who was ever-present for Leeds United last season

L This England international has been with the Red Devils since the age of 7

M The Seagulls' Premier League top scorer last season

AT THE TRAINING GROUND...

Come three o'clock on a Saturday afternoon, the fans get to see their heroes in action at Vicarage Road.

Matchday is the day the Hornets' players, manager and coaching staff are all preparing for and focusing on throughout the week. All that preparation takes places at the club's training ground, well away from the watching eyes of the thousands of fans who flock to Vicarage Road in hope of witnessing another winning performance.

The hard work begins in the summer months when the players all report back for pre-season training. The players are given a fitness programme to follow over the summer break and the first few days back at the training ground tend to involve a number of fitness tests. The results will enable the coaching and fitness staff to assess each player's condition and level of fitness to ensure they are given the right workload over pre-season, so that they are fully match fit and raring to go for the big kick-off.

A lot of the work done over the pre-season period is designed to help the players reach a level of fitness that they can maintain for the entire campaign and perform at their maximum throughout the season.

When it comes to winning football matches, it is well known that practice, dedication and preparation are all vital ingredients for success. However, in terms of strength and fitness; rest, recovery and diet also play crucial parts in a footballer's welfare. The Watford players are not only given the best of surfaces to practice on, but also given expert advice and guidance to ensure that they are fully equipped for the Premier League challenges ahead.

Technology also plays its part in helping the Watford stars perform to their maximum. Prior to taking to the training pitches, players are provided with a GPS tracking system and heart rate analysis monitors ensuring that all they do, can be measured, monitored and reviewed.

And if all goes to plan, the team's drive, commitment and meticulous preparation on the training ground during the week, will pay dividends on matchday.

WATFORD

THE LEGEND
LLOYD DOYLEY

1. A LEGEND IS BORN

A fine career which spanned 443 Watford outings started in 2001 in bizarre fashion. Called from the bench and ready to come on for his professional debut, an 18-year-old Doyley watched from the side-line as Pierre Issa - already in some discomfort following an injury suffered against Birmingham - was dropped from his stretcher. Talk about adding insult to injury!

2. BACK IN THE BIG-TIME

There were more glamorous members of Aidy Boothroyd's 2005/06 promotion-winning side, but none more reliable than Doyley. The right-back played 50 times - including all three Play-Off games - and his steadying influence at the back helped the Hornets achieve what few thought possible in re-gaining their place in the Premier League.

3. 269th TIME LUCKY!

It took a remarkable 269 games, but Doyley finally scored his first goal as Watford defeated QPR in 2009. Much to the disbelief of the Hornets' fans - who responded by singing 'We were there when Doyley scored' - the defender netted an impressive diving header at the Vicarage Road end. Cue wild celebrations!

4. TESTIMONIAL TIME

A Tottenham side featuring Gareth Bale played their part as the Hornets honoured their long-serving defender with a testimonial match. In Watford's final pre-season friendly and their first game at The Vic since the Pozzo takeover, Jermain Defoe scored the only goal on an afternoon that belonged to Doyley.

5. DOYLEY SCORES...AGAIN!

There was more than a slice of luck as his mis-struck cross unexpectedly found the top corner against Bolton in 2012, but Doyley wouldn't have minded as it was just the second goal of a Watford career which had started more than a decade earlier. It was also the last time he'd score in 449 professional matches.

KIKO FEMENÍA

WATFORD FC LADIES

Watford FC Ladies compete in the FA Women's National League South - tier three of the pyramid - under the guidance of Head Coach Armand Kavaja and has developed into a hub for female participation in the Watford community.

A growth in women's football has been building for many years and a peak audience of 11.7 million tuned in to watch England's hopes of reaching a first women's World Cup final end in a 2-1 defeat to the USA. As Grace Williams rightly pointed out, what was different was the level of new-found interest in the game. Wider interest means increased opportunity and France 2019 has provided a "huge starting point" as the club's general manager explained.

"The women's game has been growing and growing since I was a young girl and seeing what it is now from when I was playing when I was 10, 15 years old it's massively grown," Williams said. "However, I think the World Cup has made it more visual to people that perhaps weren't interested or knew much about women's football.

"Suddenly it was everywhere. We were on the front of papers, on all the news and the radio, I couldn't get away from it. That's never happened before and in that sense that's a huge starting point in so many different ways."

Golden Girls captain Helen Ward also believes the tournament has led to a change in attitude in some quarters - a change for the better. She said:

"Often I see on social media in particular if a club posts something about their women's team you get a lot of nice replies but you always get the odd idiot saying 'we don't want to know about women's football, it's as boring as this, that and the other'. But I was lucky enough to be involved in a shirt promotion with the club shop and I don't think I saw one negative response which is quite amazing."

Interest in the women's game may be at an all-time high - Williams said the Hornets are "absolutely" looking at staging another ladies fixture at Vicarage Road - but how can Watford use this to their advantage in the longer term?

"The young girls are the future of where we want to be," the former Hornets Academy and centre of excellence player responded. "If there were not people playing football then we wouldn't have a squad.

"Especially at our level and that little bit lower, they've got to have that passion to want to play because they might not have made it into an academy or a top league club.

"I think if they believe it and they keep going and you're seeing that all these players are coming up through the National League, the Championship into the WSL (Women's Super League) they can get to where they want to be and play seriously."

Danny
WELBECK
10

POSITION: **Forward**   COUNTRY: **England**   DOB: **26/11/1990**

The England international had a frustrating 2018/19 season due to injury and was picked up on a free transfer by Watford in the summer after leaving Arsenal. A product of Manchester United's Academy, the forward has won several prestigious trophies including the Premier League and FA Cup, and has represented England at the World Cup in 2014 and 2018.

Adam
MASINA
11

POSITION: **Defender**   COUNTRY: **Italy**   DOB: **02/01/1994**

The Italian full-back joined Watford from Bologna in July 2018. Despite making a name for himself in Italy with 99 appearances in Serie A, Masina could not displace José Holebas as first choice left-back last season, making eleven Premier League starts for the club and a further four in cup competitions.

Nathaniel
CHALOBAH
14

POSITION: Midfielder   **COUNTRY:** England   **DOB:** 12/12/1994

Chalobah only made 13 appearances last season, mostly down to injuries and the impressive form of Will Hughes, Étienne Capoue and Abdoulaye Doucouré. A talented and dynamic midfielder, he is the most capped player in the history of English youth football. He signed permanently for Watford in July 2017, having previously been on loan at the club in the Championship during the 2012/13 season.

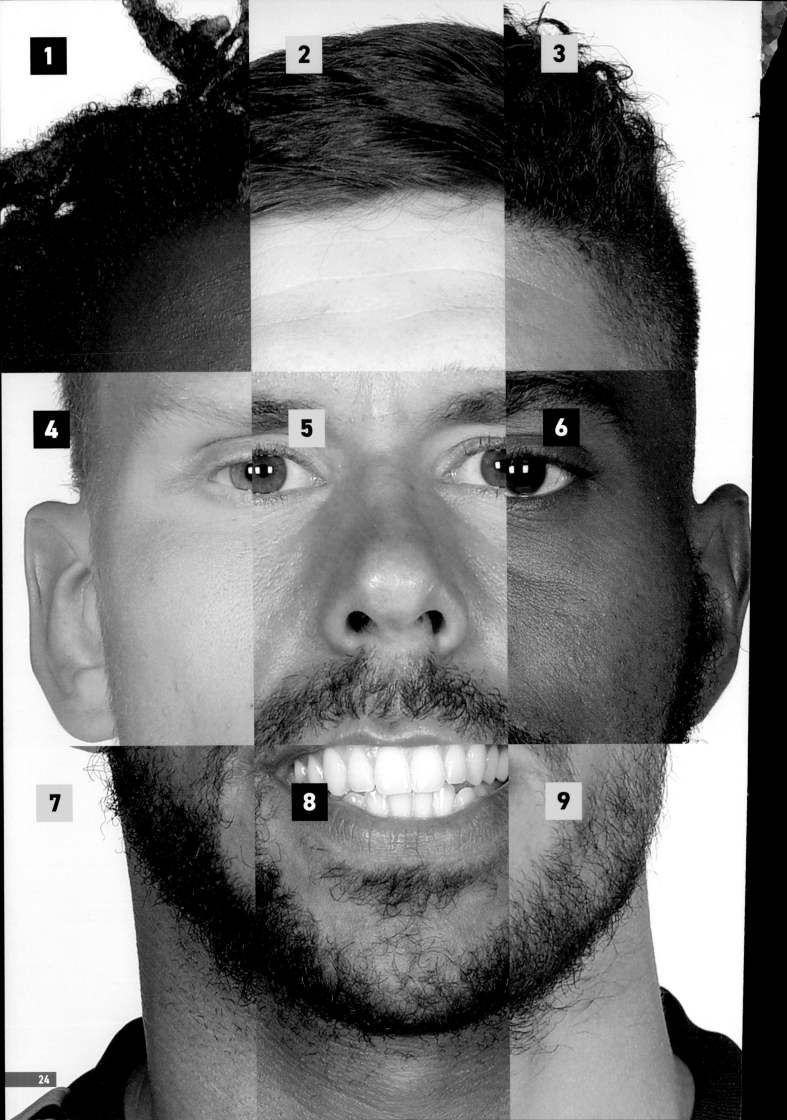

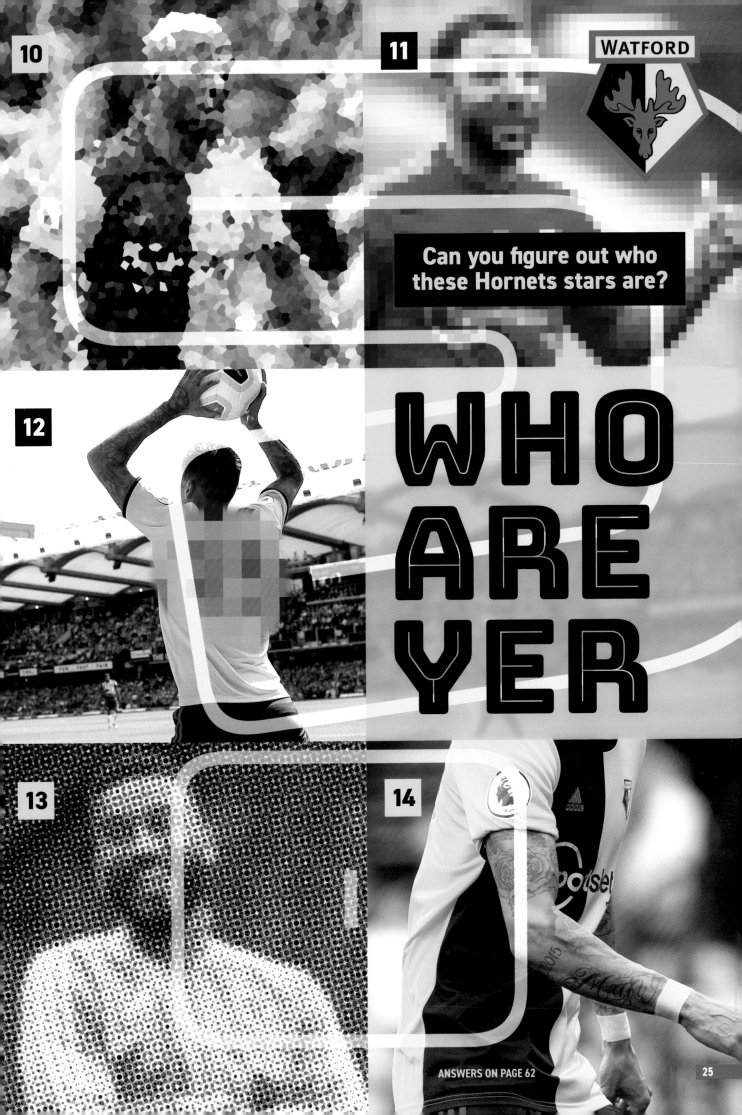

10

11

WATFORD

Can you figure out who these Hornets stars are?

WHO ARE YER

12

13

14

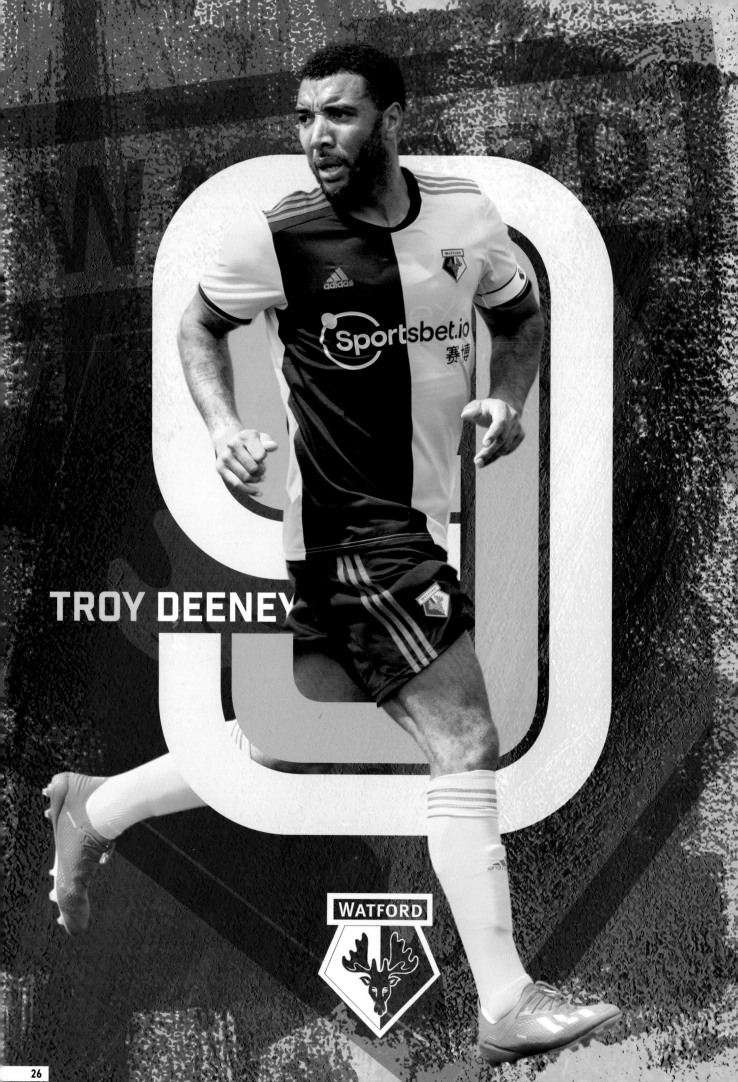

TROY DEENEY

Colour this picture of Andre Gray!

WATFORD

18

ANDRE GRAY

Sportsbet

Craig
CATHCART   15

POSITION: **Defender**   COUNTRY: **Northern Ireland**   DOB: **06/02/1989**

Having joined Watford from Blackpool, Cathcart played a key part in Watford's 2014/15 promotion season and has since adapted well to the Premier League, missing just five games last season and netting three goals. The Northern Ireland international also previously spent time at Vicarage Road, on loan from Manchester United, during the 2009/10 season.

Abdoulaye
DOUCOURÉ   16

POSITION: **Midfielder**   COUNTRY: **France**   DOB: **01/01/1993**

A combative midfielder who has also proven he has an eye for goal, Doucouré joined Watford from Rennes in January 2016, before a short loan stint at Granada. He has been an influential figure since returning, winning the 2017/18 Player of the Year award, as well as scoring five goals in 40 games last season.

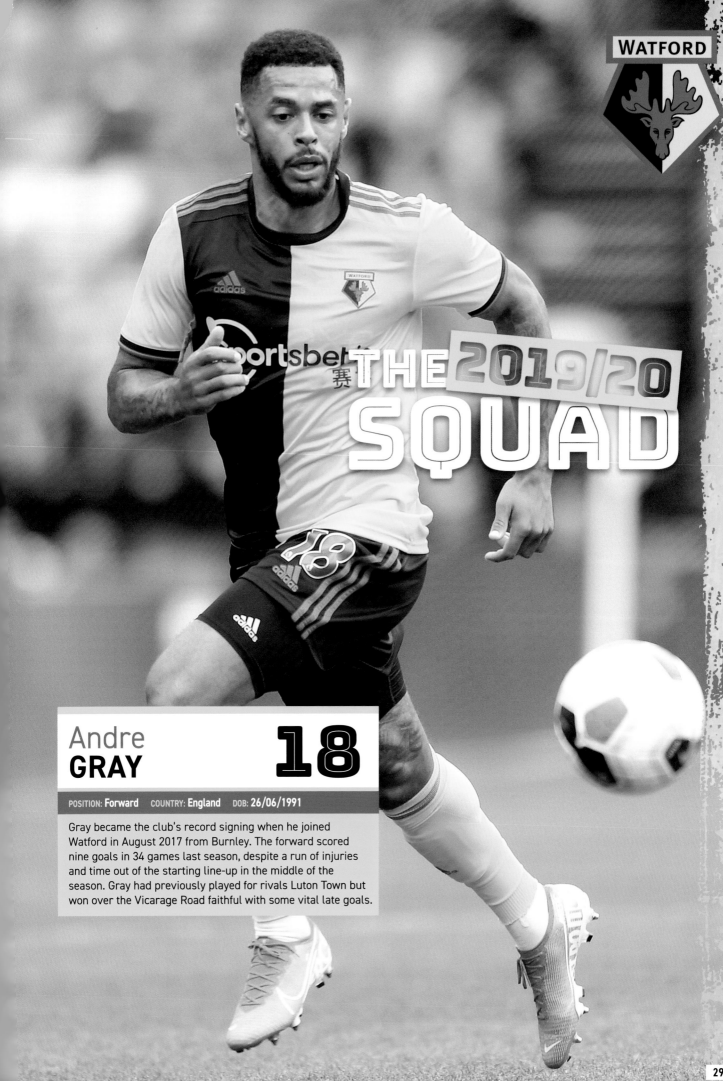

WATFORD

THE 2019/20 SQUAD

Andre GRAY

18

POSITION: **Forward**   COUNTRY: **England**   DOB: **26/06/1991**

Gray became the club's record signing when he joined Watford in August 2017 from Burnley. The forward scored nine goals in 34 games last season, despite a run of injuries and time out of the starting line-up in the middle of the season. Gray had previously played for rivals Luton Town but won over the Vicarage Road faithful with some vital late goals.

The 2018/19 season saw a number of impressive performances from the Hornets, here are three to remember...

REWIND

WATFORD 2
TOTTENHAM HOTSPUR 1

PREMIER LEAGUE · SUNDAY SEPTEMBER 2, 2018

Two sides with three wins from their opening three league fixtures met at The Vic, and it was the Hornets who ended an exciting afternoon with their 100 per cent record intact.

Tottenham looked on course for all three points when an unlucky Abdoulaye Doucouré own goal gave them the lead shortly after half-time, but two headers in the space of seven minutes from Troy Deeney and Craig Cathcart ensured Watford's best ever start to a Premier League season continued.

It was also the Hornets' first league win over Spurs since 1987, ending a run of 12 games spanning 31 years without victory over their north London opponents.

CARDIFF CITY 1
WATFORD 5

PREMIER LEAGUE · FRIDAY FEBRUARY 22, 2019

Gerard Deulofeu was the Hornets' hero in south Wales, scoring the club's first top-flight hat-trick since 1986 as a rampant Watford put five past Neil Warnock's Cardiff City.

As if firing his team into a three-goal lead wasn't enough, the former Barcelona attacker then unselfishly set up Troy Deeney to make it 4-0 before Sol Bamba netted a consolation for the Bluebirds.

Captain Deeney completed the scoring in stoppage time as the Hornets hit the target five times in a top-flight match for the first time in 32 years.

WATFORD 3
WOLVES 2 (AET)

FA CUP SEMI-FINAL · SUNDAY APRIL 7, 2019

In a true Wembley classic, Watford completed a sensational comeback from two goals down to reach their first FA Cup final since 1984 in the most dramatic fashion possible.

Matt Doherty and Raúl Jiménez goals in each half meant Wolves were well in control, but an audacious chip from substitute Gerard Deulofeu and Troy Deeney's 94th-minute penalty sent the game to extra-time.

Step forward Deulofeu, who completed his game-changing cameo by steering home a thrilling winner, setting up a showdown with Manchester City in what would be the Hornets' second ever cup final.

Answer these questions on the 2018/19 campaign and see how much attention you were paying LAST SEASON!

1. Who made the most Premier League appearances for the Hornets last season?

ANSWER

2. Who put in the most Premier League tackles last season?

ANSWER

3. How many points did Watford finish the 2018/19 season with?

ANSWER

4. How many Premier League goals did the Hornets score last season?

ANSWER

5. What was the highest home attendance of 2018/19?

ANSWER

6. Against which club did the Hornets hit five goals last season?

ANSWER

7. Who made the most Premier League passes for Watford last season?

ANSWER

8. Who beat Watford in the final of the FA Cup last season?

ANSWER

9. Who received the most yellow cards in the Premier League last season?

ANSWER

10. Who did Watford sign from Barcelona in summer 2018?

ANSWER

11. How many Premier League clean sheets did Watford keep last season?

ANSWER

12. Who top scored for the Hornets last season with ten Premier League goals?

ANSWER

ANSWERS ON PAGE 62

FAST FORWARD

There are lots of exciting games ahead for the Hornets in the second half of the 2019/20 Premier League campaign.

Here are three potential crackers...

WATFORD v EVERTON
SATURDAY FEBRUARY 1, 2020

With former Head Coach Marco Silva in charge and ex-Hornet Richarlison leading the line, Everton certainly have connections to Watford. The number of sub-plots means there will be more than just three points at stake when the Toffees visit Vicarage Road.

It was a narrow loss for the Hornets at Goodison Park earlier this season and an early Bernard goal was all that separated the teams, to the disappointment of the travelling fans. But Watford have won their last three home games against Everton and will be hoping to make it four from four.

CRYSTAL PALACE v WATFORD
SATURDAY MARCH 7, 2020

Watford beat Crystal Palace three times last season - twice in the league and once in the FA Cup quarter-final - with each fixture ending 2-1 to the Hornets. Crystal Palace will be hoping for revenge this campaign and it will be a tough trip to Selhurst Park.

The clubs have shared a lot of history in recent years too, with Crystal Palace twice beating Watford at Wembley – in the Championship Play-Off final in 2013 and the FA Cup semi-final in 2016. Both sides will be hoping for an important win as the season reaches crunch point.

WATFORD v MANCHESTER CITY
SATURDAY MAY 9, 2020

Watford played Manchester City last May in the FA Cup final at Wembley but disappointingly lost 6-0 to the domestic treble winners. Almost a year on from the historic occasion, the Hornets will be facing the reigning champions in the Premier League, hoping for a better result.

As the penultimate game of the season it could well be an important one, but the Golden Boys' loss at Wembley was their eleventh in a row against Manchester City in a spell lasting just over six years, meaning a miraculous result at Vicarage Road would be even more special.

PREMIER LEAGUE

OUR PREDICTION FOR PREMIER LEAGUE WINNERS:

CHELSEA

YOUR PREDICTION:

OUR PREDICTION FOR PREMIER LEAGUE RUNNERS-UP:

LIVERPOOL

YOUR PREDICTION:

CHAMPIONSHIP

OUR PREDICTION FOR CHAMPIONSHIP WINNERS:

DERBY COUNTY

YOUR PREDICTION:

OUR PREDICTION FOR CHAMPIONSHIP RUNNERS-UP:

CARDIFF CITY

YOUR PREDICTION:

THE FA CUP

OUR PREDICTION FOR FA CUP WINNERS:

WATFORD

YOUR PREDICTION:

OUR PREDICTION FOR FA CUP RUNNERS-UP:

TOTTENHAM HOTSPUR

YOUR PREDICTION:

EFL CUP

OUR PREDICTION FOR EFL CUP WINNERS:

NORWICH CITY

YOUR PREDICTION:

OUR PREDICTION FOR EFL CUP RUNNERS-UP:

FULHAM

YOUR PREDICTION:

2020 PREDICTIONS

WATFORD

TEAMWORK

Every Premier League team is hidden in the grid, except one!
Can you figure out which is missing?

Arsenal

Aston Villa

Bournemouth

Brighton and Hove Albion

Burnley

Chelsea

Crystal Palace

Everton

Leicester City

Liverpool

Manchester City

Manchester United

Newcastle United

Norwich City

Sheffield United

Southampton

Tottenham Hotspur

Watford

West Ham United

Wolverhampton Wanderers

```
J T S E W A K B M R R A T S T C B
E S O T E A S T O N V I L L A R Y
A Q E T S N N B H T E U F T E Y S
E B A O T A P R U V P B K Q O S D
V O J D H E S I M R D B I E V T N
I U T C A W N G E B N U C H I A Z
F R X E M R L H E Y F L K J M L P
M N J G U S I T A I Y O E A E P U
A E H O N R U O N M H X G Y P A S
O M B N I E S N F J H L N W L L A
Y O D K T R Z A N J M O D Q R A P
T U E Z E E H N O H R E T A E C Y
I T T Y D D S D R K L E S S A E T
C H I U F N J H W I S B L S P C I
R N N D A A S O I W U E F P B U C
E F U H G W H V C A H M X D V B R
T E E I F N T E H C N F C G L Y E
S P L R F O E A C D C J I E T V T
E Y T N S T G L I V E R P O O L S
C W S O S P E B T R P G N Y F K E
I W A I V M D I Y V R I B E V H H
E Z C N D A K O E H X E M V I O C
L Q W E L H R N G O M O A E C H N
S M E J K R J S E W R N R R K U A
M A N C H E S T E R U N I T E D M
J A H G U V X B N N I G G O U T H
D I X A F L W M M Y A C L N V H C
C S D O J O L E K Y Z L T B Q S X
K Q B N T W A T F O R D W S Z I P
L F B Y U H N O T P M A H T U O S
```

ANSWERS ON PAGE 62

GERARD DEULOFEU

 Middlesbrough keeper who played all 46 league games last season R

Joint Premier League top scorer last season alongside teammate Mané and Arsenal's Aubameyang

S

N France international who joined Spurs from Olympique Lyonnais in July 2019

 Nickname of Yorkshire club Barnsley T

O Goalkeeper and local lad who came through the ranks at Norwich

U The Clarets' team kit manufacturer

 Former England international in the manager's seat at Craven Cottage P

 The home of Championship new boys Charlton Athletic V

W Managed the Blades to promotion to the Premier League

Switzerland international who plays his home games at the Emirates Stadium **X**

WATFORD

2019/20 PART 2

WHO'S WHO & WHAT'S WHAT OF ENGLISH FOOTBALL?

Nottingham Forest's Argentine defensive midfielder **Y**

Z Hammers defender capped over 50 times by Argentina

ANSWERS ON PAGE 62 **37**

Domingos QUINA 20

POSITION: **Midfielder**   COUNTRY: **Portugal**   DOB: **18/11/1999**

A star of the 2018 Under-19 European Championships, Quina is an exciting young player who is looking to break into the first team. He scored two goals in 13 appearances last season, both of which were impressive efforts, and won the club's Young Player of the Season award. Signed from West Ham on deadline day in August 2018.

Will HUGHES 19

POSITION: **Midfielder**   COUNTRY: **England**   DOB: **17/04/1995**

After building up a wealth of experience with Derby in the Championship, Hughes joined Watford to play Premier League football in July 2017. Naturally a central midfielder, he excelled on the right last season thanks to a hard-working attitude. The former England Under-21 international scored three goals in 40 appearances for the Hornets in 2018/19.

THE 2019/20 SQUAD

Kiko FEMENÍA

21

POSITION: **Defender**   COUNTRY: **Spain**   DOB: **02/02/1991**

A right-back who is also comfortable playing on the wing, Femenía joined the Golden Boys from Alaves in July 2017. He likes to get forward and even bagged himself a goal last season, rounding off the scoring in a 4-1 win against Fulham in April. His game-time is shared with Daryl Janmaat at right-back, and he made 34 appearances last campaign.

Isaac SUCCESS

22

POSITION: **Forward**   COUNTRY: **Nigeria**   DOB: **07/01/1996**

Success joined the Hornets in 2016 and has regularly appeared off the bench during his time at the club, making 35 total appearances last season. A strong and powerful winger, the 23-year-old scored in League Cup games against Reading and Tottenham last campaign, as well as bagging the second goal in an FA Cup game against Newcastle.

BURNLEY
TURF MOOR
CAPACITY: 22,546

MANCHESTER CITY
ETIHAD STADIUM
CAPACITY: 55,097

MANCHESTER UTD
OLD TRAFFORD
CAPACITY: 76,000

EVERTON
GOODISON PARK
CAPACITY: 39,572

LIVERPOOL
ANFIELD
CAPACITY: 54,074

LEICESTER CITY
KING POWER STADIUM
CAPACITY: 32,312

WOLVES
MOLINEUX STADIUM
CAPACITY: 31,700

ASTON VILLA
VILLA PARK
CAPACITY: 42,785

WATFORD
VICARAGE ROAD
CAPACITY: 21,577

SOUTHAMPTON
ST MARY'S STADIUM
CAPACITY: 32,384

BOURNEMOUTH
VITALITY STADIUM
CAPACITY: 11,329

NEWCASTLE UTD
ST JAMES' PARK
CAPACITY: 52,405

WATFORD

PREMIER LEAGUE GROUNDS 2019/20

Get a quick look at where the Hornets will be heading this season to take on their rivals.

Tick off the grounds once we've visited!

SHEFFIELD UTD
BRAMALL LANE
CAPACITY: 32,702

NORWICH CITY
CARROW ROAD
CAPACITY: 27,244

ARSENAL
EMIRATES STADIUM
CAPACITY: 60,260

TOTTENHAM HOTSPUR
TOTTENHAM HOTSPUR STADIUM
CAPACITY: 62,062

WEST HAM UTD
LONDON STADIUM
CAPACITY: 66,000

CRYSTAL PALACE
SELHURST PARK
CAPACITY: 25,456

CHELSEA
STAMFORD BRIDGE
CAPACITY: 41,631

BRIGHTON & HA
AMERICAN EXPRESS COMMUNITY STADIUM
CAPACITY: 30,666

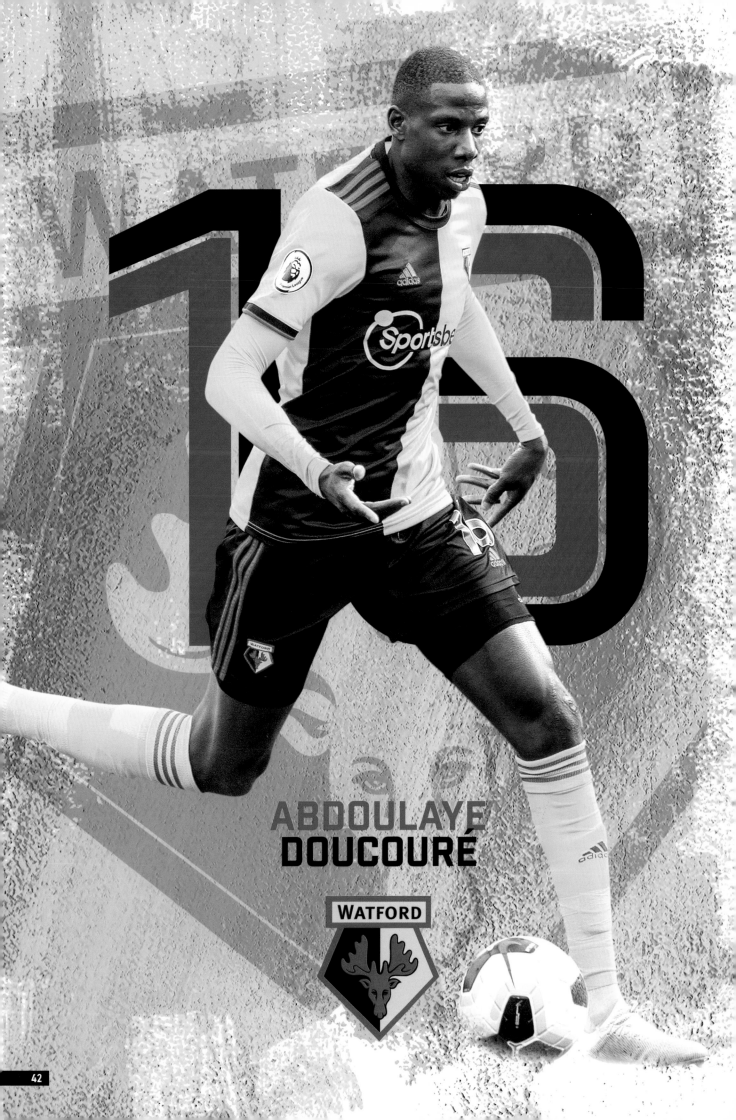

ABDOULAYE
DOUCOURÉ

THE LEGEND
TOMMY MOONEY

1. SCORE SETTLED

Having arrived on loan from Southend in March 1994, Mooney had a point to prove when his parent club visited a month later. He was a man on a mission, scoring the first of 65 Watford goals in a 3-0 win and proving the Shrimpers' loss was definitely the Hornets' gain. He signed permanently that summer, and the rest was history.

2. BACK TO BASICS

Usually a forward player, Graham Taylor switched Mooney to a surprise defensive role for the 1997/98 season and it worked a treat. Playing in a back-three alongside Keith Millen and Robert Page, he excelled as Watford clinched the Division Two title and automatic promotion. A tactical masterstroke from GT!

3. MAN OF THE MOMENT

He didn't open his 1998/99 account until February, but the floodgates opened and Mooney's seven goals in the final seven league games inspired Watford to a late Play-Off push. It was just the tonic the Hornets needed, and they went on to achieve a second successive promotion via Play-Off wins over Birmingham and Bolton.

4. HISTORY MAKER

A boyhood Liverpool fan, scoring a winner in front of the Kop was a dream turned reality for Mooney, who bagged the game's only goal in early 1999/2000 to defeat a team featuring Carragher, Gerrard and Fowler. It was Watford's first win since promotion and their only victory at Anfield in 15 attempts prior to the start of 2019/20.

5. SIGNING OFF IN STYLE

Comfortably his most prolific campaign at Watford, Mooney scored an impressive 22 goals as the Hornets returned to life in Division One. In what turned out to be his final season at The Vic, Mooney scored doubles against Notts County, Grimsby, West Brom, Wimbledon and Nottingham Forest and was rightly named 2000/01 Player of the Season.

ANSWERS ON PAGE 62

WATFORD

Ismaïla
SARR
23

POSITION: **Forward**   COUNTRY: **Senegal**   DOB: **25/02/1998**

Sarr became Watford's record signing when he joined from Rennes in the summer. The forward scored 13 times last season, including a goal in the Europa League against Arsenal and one in the African Nations Cup against Kenya for Senegal. Sarr can play as a striker or out wide but tends to prefer playing on the right. He scored on his first start in the League Cup win over Coventry.

THE 2019/20 SQUAD

Tom
DELE-BASHIRU
24

POSITION: **Midfielder**   COUNTRY: **Nigeria**   DOB: **17/09/1999**

The young Dele-Bashiru joined the Hornets in the summer, having previously been part of Manchester City's youth set up. The midfielder has represented England at Under-16 level and Nigeria at Under-20, scoring a goal at the 2019 FIFA U-20 World Cup in Poland.

José
HOLEBAS
25

POSITION: **Defender**   COUNTRY: **Greece**   DOB: **27/06/1984**

An experienced defender, Holebas notched an impressive three goals and six assists last season, from 28 appearances. The Greek left-back signed from Roma in 2015 and became a popular figure at Watford, reaching 100 Premier League appearances on the final day of 2018/19 season.

Christian KABASELE 27

POSITION: **Defender** COUNTRY: **Belgium** DOB: **24/02/1991**

The Belgium international joined from Genk in 2016 and has made over 50 appearances for the Hornets at centre-back. Born in the Democratic Republic of Congo, Kabasele started his career as a striker and his eye for goal is evident, as he bagged five goals in his first three seasons for Watford.

Ben FOSTER 26

POSITION: **Goalkeeper** COUNTRY: **England** DOB: **03/04/1983**

The former England shot-stopper made a welcome return to Vicarage Road in July 2018, joining from West Brom and starting every game in the league last campaign. Foster had previously been at the club on loan from Manchester United during the 2005/06 and 2006/07 seasons, when the Hornets last gained promotion to the Premier League.

THE LEGEND
HEIÐAR HELGUSON

1. INSTANT IMPACT

Signed for a club record £1.5 million, Helguson was thrown straight into the team just a few days later and enjoyed a dream debut, scoring a trademark header as Watford overturned a two-goal deficit to peg Liverpool back. Graham Taylor's men ended up losing 3-2, but a genuine new Hornets hero had been born.

2. UP FOR THE CUP

In one of his finest Watford outings, Helguson single-handedly ran a defence containing Marcel Desailly and William Gallas ragged as Watford held Chelsea to a shock 2-2 draw in the FA Cup. The Icelander scored after five minutes and, playing as a lone striker, was a constant menace for the expensively-assembled Blues. A vintage Helguson performance.

3. QUARTER-FINAL DOUBLE

Another stellar cup performance saw Helguson bag a brace in a League Cup quarter-final against Portsmouth. The forward showed poacher's instincts to convert from a Neal Ardley free-kick and then a Jermaine Darlington cross, before Bruce Dyer capped off a 3-0 win. The result sent the Hornets to a prestigious semi-final against Liverpool.

4. A GOLDEN SEASON

Helguson's final season in his first spell with the Hornets was his best in a Watford shirt. As well as winning the prestigious Player of the Season award at the end of the 2004/05 campaign, Helguson picked up the Goal of the Season and Display of the Season awards too. The forward bagged 20 goals in all competitions before signing for Fulham in the summer.

5. THE SECOND COMING

A return to Vicarage Road was on the cards for Helguson in 2009, in the form of a loan move from Queens Park Rangers. The Icelander made an instant impact again on his second debut, coming off the bench to score twice in 17 minutes against Leicester City. He bagged eleven goals during the season and will forever be remembered fondly by the Vicarage Road faithful.

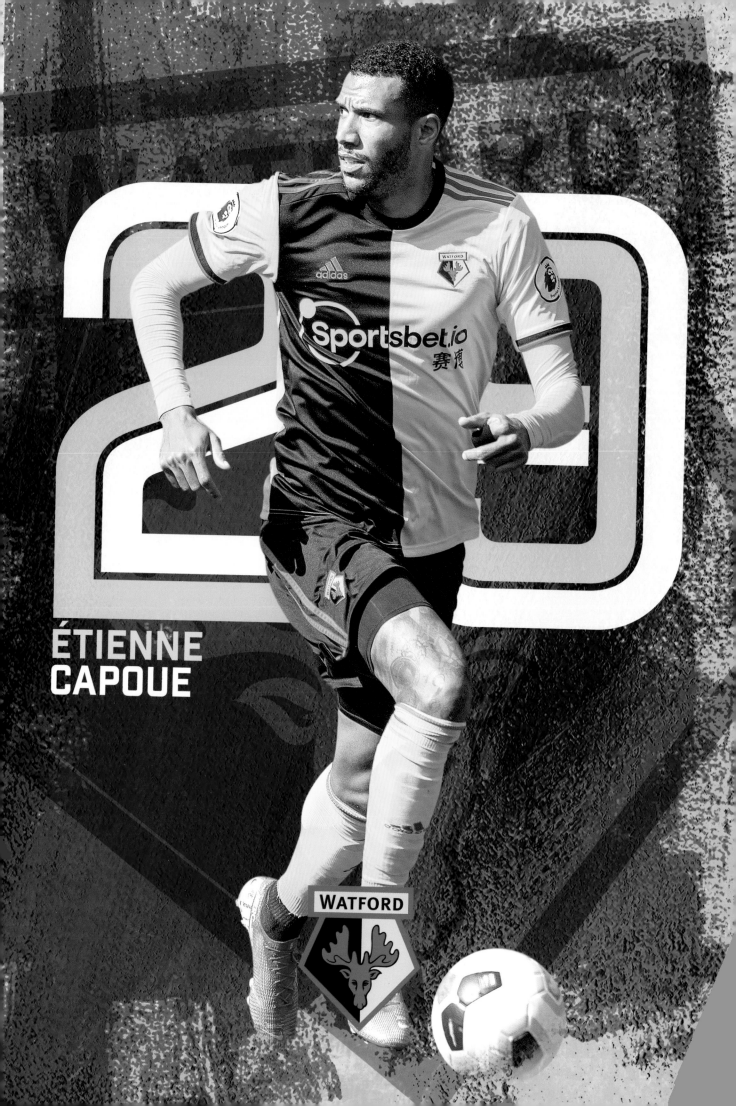

ÉTIENNE
CAPOUE

PREMIER
LEAGUE 2019/2

ARSENAL

ASTON VILLA

BOURNEMOU

BRIGHTON & HA

BURNLEY

CHELSEA

YSTAL PALACE

EVERTON

LEICESTER CITY

In a yellow and
black world, get
to know your rivals
in full Premier
League colour!

LIVERPOOL

MANCHESTER CITY

MANCHESTER UNITED

NEWCASTLE UNITED

NORWICH CITY

SHEFFIELD UNITED

SOUTHAMPTON

TOTTENHAM HOTSPUR

WATFORD

WEST HAM UNITED

WOLVES

WATFORD

ÉTIENNE
CAPOUE

2018/19

PLAYER
OF THE
SEASON

51

What a season 2018/19 was for Étienne Capoue.

The French midfielder convincingly topped the supporters' vote and was crowned Graham Taylor OBE Player of the Season at the club's prestigious End of Season Awards Evening at Wembley Stadium, and rightly so.

Beating off strong competition from closest challengers Ben Foster (second) and José Holebas (third), Capoue emerged as the leading candidate after delivering what he described as his best season so far after more than a decade in the professional game.

A midfielder who already possessed bundles of technical ability and oozed class operating alongside compatriot Abdoulaye Doucouré in the centre of the Hornets' park, Capoue added defensive nous and a genuine work ethic to his game under Javi Gracia last season.

No player made more interceptions in the 2018/19 Premier League campaign than Capoue's 86, and he also chipped in with important goals against QPR and Crystal Palace during Watford's incredible run to the FA Cup final.

Match of the Day pundit Danny Murphy even described Capoue's central midfield partnership with 2017/18 Player of the Season Doucouré as the best there was in the Premier League. High praise indeed, and not unwarranted.

One of the more experienced players in the Golden Boys' changing room, former Tottenham and Toulouse man Capoue was handed the captain's armband for matches against Manchester City and Southampton, underlining the Frenchman's growth in maturity since his arrival at Vicarage Road in 2015.

YOUNG PLAYER
OF THE SEASON

DOMINGOS QUINA

Domingos Quina started life with Watford by turning up unannounced on transfer deadline day in August 2018, and by the end of his first year at The Vic he was picking up the trophy for Young Player of the Season.

That snap decision to offer the highly-rated Portugal Under-20 international a contract was more than vindicated as the former West Ham, Chelsea and Benfica youngster eased into life with the Hornets, scoring a stunning Goal of the Season contender during his debut at Reading in the League Cup.

Injury restricted the midfielder's game-time during the latter stages of the season, but we'd seen more than enough of Quina to know that Watford had a seriously bright prospect on their hands.

Étienne
CAPOUE
29

POSITION: **Midfielder**   COUNTRY: **France**   DOB: **11/07/1988**

The box-to-box midfielder signed for Watford from Tottenham Hotspur in 2015, having struggled to establish himself as a starter for the North London side despite impressing in his native Ligue 1. Capoue found a new lease of life at Vicarage Road, commanding midfields, breaking up play and chipping in with goals. He was last season's Player of the Year.

Pontus
DAHLBERG
30

POSITION: **Goalkeeper**   COUNTRY: **Sweden**   DOB: **21/01/1999**

Formerly of IFK Göteborg, Dahlberg spent last season learning from the experienced pair of Ben Foster and Heurelho Gomes. He arrived in January 2018, before going back on loan to the Swedish club for six months. It was at Göteborg where Dahlberg caught the eye over 47 appearances, one of which was in the Europa League.

Daniel **BACHMANN** 35

POSITION: **Goalkeeper**   COUNTRY: **Austria**   DOB: **09/07/1994**

Bachmann joined the Hornets in July 2017, having previously been at Stoke City, and spent last season on loan at Scottish side Kilmarnock. He was first choice in goal for the Scottish Premier League side. The goalkeeper has performed at youth level for Austria's national team.

Dimitri **FOULQUIER** 36

POSITION: **Defender**   COUNTRY: **Guadeloupe**   DOB: **23/03/1993**

Having signed for Watford in 2017, Foulquier has since been playing first team football at Strasbourg and Getafe and even scored three goals in La Liga last season as his side narrowly missed out on Champions League qualification. The full-back played for France's national team at youth levels and has since appeared for Guadeloupe's senior side.

THE 2019/20 SQUAD

Roberto **PEREYRA** 37

POSITION: **Midfielder**   COUNTRY: **Argentina**   DOB: **07/01/1991**

The former Juventus man and Argentina international proved himself an exciting addition to the Premier League since arriving at Watford in the summer of 2016. Last season the versatile midfielder scored six goals in 36 appearances, and he is loved by fans for his exciting and dynamic attacking play.

DANNY
WELBECK

WATFORD

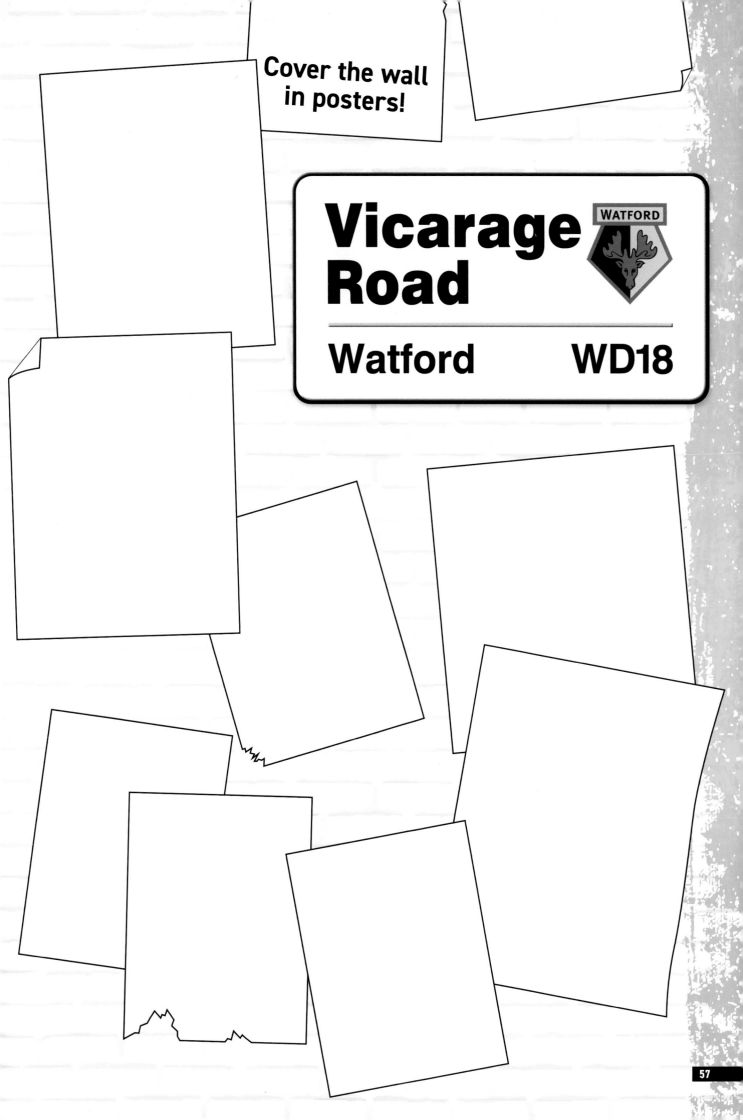

Cover the wall in posters!

Vicarage Road

Watford WD18

WATFORD

Watford have boasted a wealth of talent over the years! Here is our...

HORNETS DREAM TEAM

...see if you agree!

GOALKEEPER

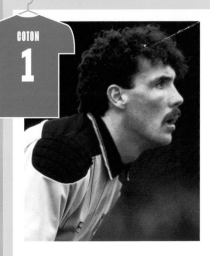

COTON 1

TONY COTON

In his six seasons with Watford, including four in the top-flight, Coton showed impeccable goalkeeping ability, winning the Player of the Season trophy an unprecedented three times.

RIGHT-BACK

GIBBS 2

NIGEL GIBBS

Gibbs made over 400 appearances across 18 seasons for Watford. A true one-club man, only Luther Blissett and Duncan Welbourne made more Football League outings for the Hornets than the full-back.

MIDFIELDER

JOHNSON 6

RICHARD JOHNSON

Aussie Johnson ventured to England as a teenager dreaming of a career in football. He ended up dominating midfields for Watford during the 1990s, banging in more than a few spectacular goals along the way.

RIGHT-WING

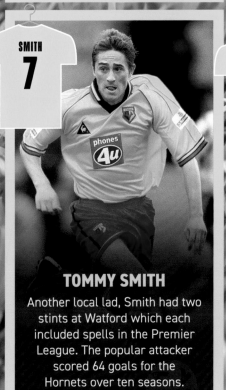

SMITH 7

TOMMY SMITH

Another local lad, Smith had two stints at Watford which each included spells in the Premier League. The popular attacker scored 64 goals for the Hornets over ten seasons.

MIDFIELDER

JACKETT 8

KENNY JACKETT

Wales international Jackett played in both defence and midfield for Watford, making over 400 appearances during the 1980s. He even managed the club during the 1996/97 season, kickstarting his career as a gaffer.

YOUR CHOICE

CENTRE-BACK

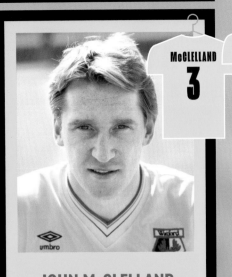

McCLELLAND
3

JOHN McCLELLAND

The towering Northern Ireland international was a rock in the heart of Watford's defence in the 1980s, leading from the back with a composed playing style and surprising pace.

CENTRE-BACK

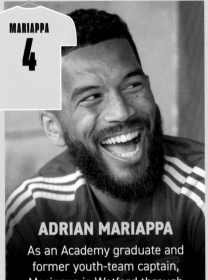

MARIAPPA
4

ADRIAN MARIAPPA

As an Academy graduate and former youth-team captain, Mariappa is Watford through and through. The athletic defender left the Hornets in 2012 after seven seasons but made his homecoming in the Premier League in 2016.

LEFT-BACK

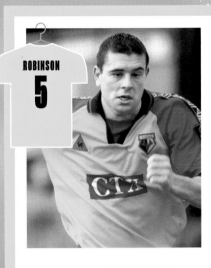

ROBINSON
5

PAUL ROBINSON

Born and raised in Watford, the robust full-back played a big part in the Hornets' rise through the divisions to the Premier League in the late 1990s under Graham Taylor.

STRIKER

DEENEY
9

TROY DEENEY

The captain has led his team to promotion, an FA Cup final and scored over 100 goals including a historic dramatic winner against Leicester City in the 2013 Play-Off semi-final.

STRIKER

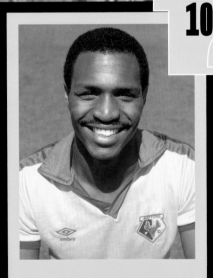

BLISSETT
10

LUTHER BLISSETT

With the most goals (186) and appearances (503) for the club, Blissett is truly Mr Watford, playing for the club through all four divisions of English football.

LEFT-WING

BARNES
11

JOHN BARNES

Widely regarded as one of the greatest ever Watford players, Barnes dazzled defences as a winger for the Hornets in the top flight and for England's national team before joining Liverpool.

TOP 10

MOMENTS OF THIS YEAR

1.
2.
3.
4.
5.
6.
7.
8.
9.
10.

MY TOP 10...

FOOTBALLERS OF ALL TIME

1.
2.
3.
4.
5.
6.
7.
8.
9.
10.

MY TOP 10...

HORNETS MEMORIES

1.
2.
3.
4.
5.
6.
7.
8.
9.
10.

MY TOP 10...

RESOLUTIONS FOR 2020

1.
2.
3.
4.
5.
6.
7.
8.
9.
10.

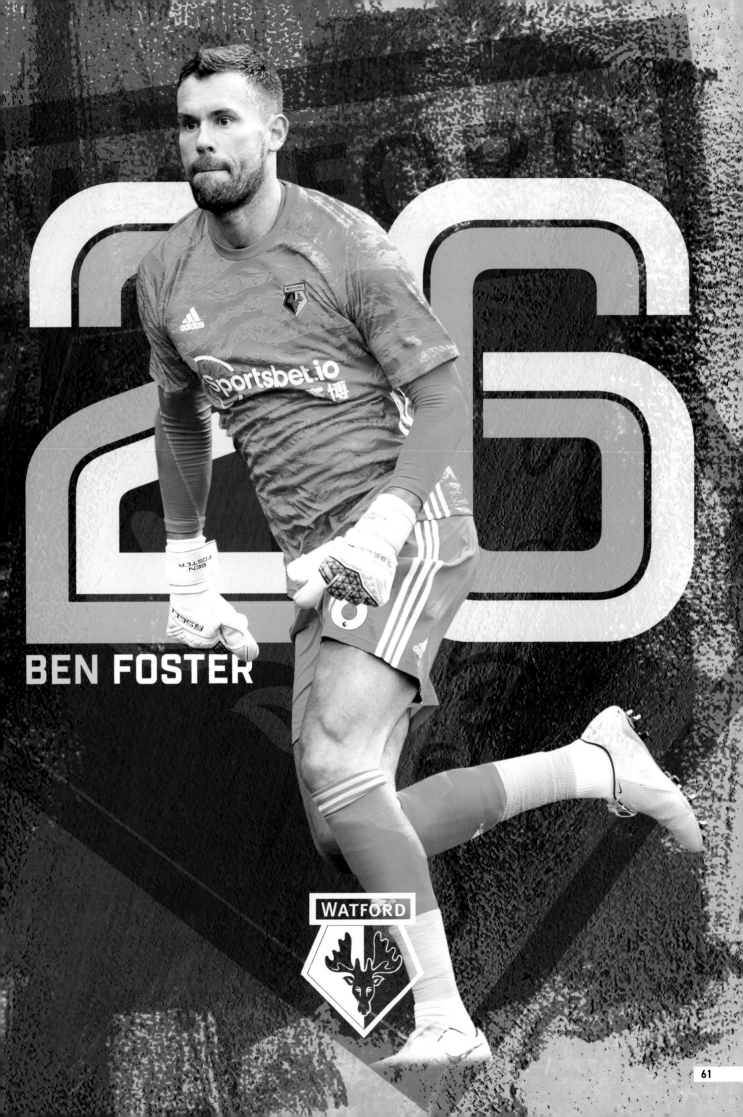

BEN FOSTER

WATFORD

ANSWERS

PAGE 14 · A-Z PART ONE

A. César Azpilicueta. B. Bristol City.
C. Matty Cash. D. Harlee Dean.
E. The Eagles. F. Thomas Frank, Brentford.
G. Goodison Park. H. Neil Harris.
I. Kelechi Iheanacho. J. Gabriel Jesus.
K. Mateusz Klich. L. Jesse Lingard.
M. Glenn Murray.

PAGE 24 · WHO ARE YER?

1. Domingos Quina. 2. Craig Cathcart.
3. Adam Masina. 4. Pontus Dahlberg.
5. Ben Foster. 6. Dimitri Foulquier.
7. Andre Gray. 8. Étienne Capoue.
9. Kiko Femenía. 10. Isaac Success.
11. Troy Deeney. 12. José Holebas.
13. Adrian Mariappa. 14. Roberto Pereyra.

PAGE 31 · REWIND

1. Ben Foster, 38 appearances.
2. Etienne Capoue, 90 tackles.
3. 50. 4. 52. 5. 20,540 v Liverpool,
24 November 2018, Premier League.
6. Cardiff City. 7. Abdoulaye Doucouré,
1,942 passes. 8. Manchester City.
9. Etienne Capoue, 14 yellow cards.
10. Gerard Deulofeu. 11. 7.
12. Gerard Deulofeu.

PAGE 34 · TEAMWORK

Sheffield United.

PAGE 36 · A-Z PART TWO

N. Tanguy Ndombele. O. Aston Oxborough.
P. Scott Parker. Q. Domingos Quina.
R. Darren Randolph. S. Mo Salah.
T. The Tykes. U. Umbro. V. The Valley.
W. Chris Wilder. X. Granit Xhaka.
Y. Claudio Yacob. Z. Pablo Zabaleta.

PAGE 44 · HEY REF

1. Direct free kick. 2. Indirect free kick.
3. Yellow card – Caution.
4. Red card – Sending off. 5. Obstruction.
6. Substitution. 7. Offside/foul. 8. Penalty.
9. Offside location. 10. Play on.